MW00534919

Octopuses

by Joanne Mattern

BELLWETHER MEDIA • MINNEAPOLIS, MN

Blastoff! Readers are carefully developed by literacy experts to build reading stamina and move students toward fluency by combining standards-based content with developmentally appropriate text.

Level 1 provides the most support through repetition of high-frequency words, light text, predictable sentence patterns, and strong visual support.

Level 2 offers early readers a bit more challenge through varied sentences, increased text load, and text-supportive special features.

Level 3 advances early-fluent readers toward fluency through increased text load, less reliance on photos, advancing concepts, longer sentences, and more complex special features.

★ **Blastoff! Universe**

Reading Level

Grade **K**

Grades **1–3**

Grade **4**

This edition first published in 2021 by Bellwether Media, Inc.

No part of this publication may be reproduced in whole or in part without written permission of the publisher. For information regarding permission, write to Bellwether Media, Inc., Attention: Permissions Department, 6012 Blue Circle Drive, Minnetonka, MN 55343.

Library of Congress Cataloging-in-Publication Data

Names: Mattern, Joanne, 1963- author.
Title: Octopuses / by Joanne Mattern.
Description: Minneapolis, MN : Bellwether Media, 2021. | Series: Blastoff! readers: the world's smartest animals | Includes bibliographical references and index. | Audience: Ages 5-8 | Audience: Grades 2-3 | Summary: "Simple text and full-color photography introduce beginning readers to octopuses. Developed by literacy experts for students in kindergarten through third grade"-- Provided by publisher.
Identifiers: LCCN 2019059264 (print) | LCCN 2019059265 (ebook) | ISBN 9781644872413 (library binding) | ISBN 9781618919991 (ebook)
Subjects: LCSH: Octopuses--Behavior--Juvenile literature. | Animal intelligence--Juvenile literature.
Classification: LCC QL430.3.O2 M39 2021 (print) | LCC QL430.3.O2 (ebook) | DDC 594/.561513--dc23
LC record available at https://lccn.loc.gov/2019059264
LC ebook record available at https://lccn.loc.gov/2019059265

Editor: Betsy Rathburn   Designer: Jeffrey Kollock

Printed in the United States of America, North Mankato, MN.

Table of Contents

Big Brains

Octopuses are **cephalopods**. They have soft bodies and eight arms.

These **invertebrates** have no backbones. They swim through oceans all over the world.

Octopuses have large brains.
Each of their arms has its own
nerve cells. These are like
smaller brains.

Brain Size

about
1,400
grams

about
1
gram

human

octopus

Large brains make octopuses **intelligent**. They help octopuses use tools and **communicate**!

Octopuses use their intelligence to survive in the ocean. These smart swimmers use tools. They use rocks to build shelters.

Octopuses also use shells as tools. They squeeze inside to hide from **predators**!

Octopuses can change color and **texture**. This helps them blend in with their surroundings. They cannot be spotted by predators.

Their colors also help them talk to other octopuses. Some colors help octopuses find **mates**!

mates

Octopuses often travel far from home to hunt. Their intelligence helps them on their journeys.

Octopus Skills

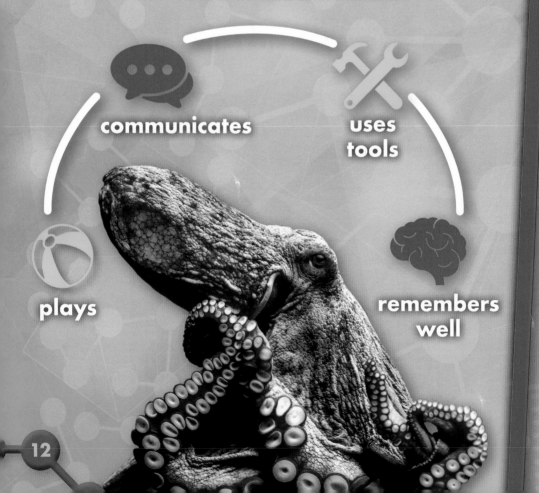

communicates

uses tools

plays

remembers well

These creatures easily **navigate** the open ocean. They remember **landmarks** to find their way home!

Learning About Octopuses

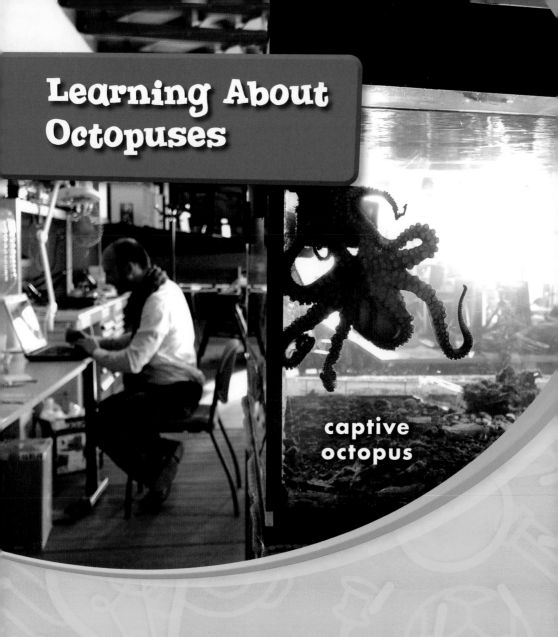

captive
octopus

Scientists study **captive** octopuses.
They learn how octopuses play.

In one study, scientists dropped a plastic bottle into an **aquarium** tank. Octopuses shot jets of water at it!

Other studies show how octopuses solve problems. One showed that octopuses can open jars to get food.

Amazing Octopus

Name
- Inky

Species
- New Zealand octopus

Famous For
- Pushed the lid off his tank, crawled across the floor, and escaped through a pipe to the sea

Octopuses can also open their tanks.
One snuck into other tanks to eat fish.
Then it went back to its own tank!

Scientists do **experiments** with octopuses, too. In one, scientists put food in a maze. They tested whether octopuses could find the food. Later, they changed the maze. The octopuses knew they were in a different maze!

Octopus Study

Question

Can octopuses solve problems?

Process

1. Scientists placed a fish in a closed jar.

2. The scientists cut a hole in the jar. It was big enough for the octopus to touch the fish.

What Happened?

- The octopus could not pull the fish out of the jar.

- The octopus used its strength to pull off the top of the jar.

Answer

- Octopuses can solve problems.

Octopuses are very different from humans. But they are very smart.

Scientists study these creatures
to learn about animal brains.
Humans can learn a lot
from octopuses!

Glossary

aquarium—a place where ocean animals are kept and shown

captive—captured and held away from home

cephalopods—animals that have excellent eyesight, ink sacs, and muscular arms with suckers; cuttlefish, octopuses, and squids are types of cephalopods.

communicate—to share thoughts and feelings using sounds, faces, and actions

experiments—tests used to try new ideas or answer questions

intelligent—able to learn or understand

invertebrates—animals without backbones

landmarks—objects that mark the way

mates—partners

navigate—to find the way from place to place

nerve cells—parts of the body that send information to the brain from other parts of the body

predators—animals that hunt other animals for food

texture—the way something looks or feels

To Learn More

AT THE LIBRARY

Montgomery, Sy. *Inky's Amazing Escape: How A Very Smart Octopus Found His Way Home.* New York, N.Y.: Simon & Schuster Books for Young Readers, 2018.

Schuh, Mari. *The Supersmart Octopus.* Minneapolis, Minn.: Lerner Publications, 2019.

Shaffer, Lindsay. *Octopuses.* Minneapolis, Minn.: Bellwether Media, 2020.

ON THE WEB

FACTSURFER

Factsurfer.com gives you a safe, fun way to find more information.

1. Go to www.factsurfer.com.

2. Enter "octopuses" into the search box and click 🔍.

3. Select your book cover to see a list of related content.

Index

The images in this book are reproduced through the courtesy of: Andrea Izzotti, front cover, pp. 1, 23; Rich Carey, pp. 3, 12, 13, 19; Richard Whitcombe, pp. 4, 5, 20, 21; Rostislav Ageev, p. 5; Shane Gross, pp. 6, 7; Nicolas_photo, pp. 8, 9; SergeUWPhoto, p. 9; Severin Benz, p. 10; Dario Sabljak, pp. 10, 11; Olga Visavi, p. 12; Laura Lezza/ Getty Images, pp. 14, 15; Bildagentur Zoonar GmbH, p. 15; Fred Bavendam/ SuperStock, p. 16; Gen_Shtab, pp. 16, 17; pr2is, p. 18; Yellowj, p. 19.